E·Z Bock's Best

Volume VI

CONTENTS

Carl Farrer

Austin, Texas

Spring, 2009

Dear Fred:

I was asked (*begged!*) to write this foreword by your son, Stephen, to whom you could never say "No" - so how could I?

I remember the first time I ever saw you. You opened the door of Manna Music at Crossroads of the World in Hollywood and said with outstretched arms, "*Here I am!*" I discovered that from that moment to this, even as I write, that you were and still are the wittiest person ever - clever and as fast as Chopin's Minute Waltz played in 30 seconds. What fun we had trying to top each other. I remember once, I took a gift card inscribed, "To You While You Are In The Service," to the Bel Air Presbyterian Church where you were organist, gave the card to the usher and asked him to put it in front of you while you played for the Sunday morning service. You nearly dropped a sixteenth note and your left foot slipped off the pedal. One for me! But not for long. You and your irrepressible wife, Lois, set me up with a surprise birthday party, inviting my best friends and including in the invitation to bring an outrageous gift. None, of course, surpassed the one from you and Lois: a ***double-album*** of *It's A Small World*, as performed at Disneyland on their famous ride of the same name. And, of course, you knew how much I hated that song. One for you (and Lois)!

All those wonderful years. All that beautiful music. All those great friends. In a store today I found a copy of *Hymns For The Family of God* that you compiled and which is now on the backs of pews in thousands and thousands of churches of many denominations all over the world. I heard you laugh as I pulled it off the shelf at the... Thrift Store. Maybe that's one for both of us!

You left us abundantly blessed with your music. And what you must have taken with you? I can just see piles and piles of boxes all over heaven marked Fred Bock's Good Deeds and Other Funny Stuff.

Oh yeah, about this piano book. You'd be really pleased how Lloyd Larson has kept your unique harmonies and flavors while simplifying these arrangements for mere mortals. He has done a great job, Fred. Like you, he has the gift of making complicated things seem easy.

Now, if only there was a way to do that with missing you?

Carl Farrer

Carl Farrer

WHAT A FRIEND WE HAVE IN JESUS

CHARLES CONVERSE
Arranged by FRED BOCK
Adapted by LLOYD LARSON

15
18
21
24
f
27

30
mp
34
f
37
mf
40
very gently
mp
p
43
ten.
mf
ten.
mp
pp
Ped

GRACE GREATER THAN OUR SIN

DANIEL B. TOWNER
Arranged by FRED BOCK
Adapted by LLOYD LARSON

Warmly and tenderly (♩ = ca. 80)

19
23
27
31
35

39
f
44
48
52
cresc. poco a poco
rit.
56
sub. p
mp

THE OLD RUGGED CROSS

GEORGE BENNARD
Arranged by FRED BOCK
Adapted by LLOYD LARSON

17
21
lightly rhythmic
mp
25
mf
29
stronger
mp
f
33
ten.
mp
ten.

37
40
mp
43
mf
f
46
1.
2.
mf
mf
p
Ped.
Ped.

BE STILL AND KNOW

Traditional Melody
Arranged by FRED BOCK
Adapted by LLOYD LARSON

17
21
f
mp
25
mf
29
33

37
f
41
mf
45
Stronger and broader
f
49
53
ten.
ten.
sub. p

57
ten.
mf
ten.
60
63
mp
66
mf
69
mf
mp
dim.
pp

PRAISE TO THE LORD, THE ALMIGHTY

LOBE DEN HERREN
Arranged by FRED BOCK
Adapted by LLOYD LARSON

15
mf
mp
19
23
f
27
31

34
mf
37
mp
mf
40
cresc.
f
44
p
mf
legato
mp
48
p

52
mp
mf
f
cresc. e rit.
ff
56
Full and strong
59
62
mf
65
lightly

68
mf
mp
71
74
77
79
ff
R.H.

WONDROUS LOVE

American Folk Melody
Arranged by FRED BOCK
Adapted by LLOYD LARSON

Moderately, freely

13
mf
rit.
mf
a tempo
16
19
f
22
25

28
broaden
31
R.H.
L.H.
p
R.H.
mp
R.H.
L.H.
34
mf
37
mp
40
mp
pp
mf
mp

I HAVE DECIDED TO FOLLOW JESUS

Indian Folk Tune
Arranged by FRED BOCK
Adapted by LLOYD LARSON

14
18
mf
22
26
no rit.
cresc. poco a poco
pp
f
p
30
bring out melody notes
pp
l.h.
mf

LEAD ME, LORD

SAMUEL WESLEY
Arranged by FRED BOCK
Adapted by LLOYD LARSON

14
17
20
23
rit.
mf
a tempo
26

29
32
35
f
38
pp
41

44
47
50
cresc.
54
ten.
f
sub. p
ten.
57
mp
p
ten.
ten.
pp

JESUS, THE VERY THOUGHT OF THEE

JOHN B. DYKES
Arranged by FRED BOCK
Adapted by LLOYD LARSON

17
mf
21
25
29
ten.
ten.
mf
33

37
40
43
46
49
dim.

I SURRENDER ALL

WINFIELD S. WEEDEN
Arranged by FRED BOCK
Adapted by LLOYD LARSON

Gently (♩ = ca. 76)

17
21
mf
25
29
33
gradual cresc.

36
ff
39
f
42
mp poco accel.
mf
f
45
rit.
mp
mf
ten.
ten.
48
p
pp
r.h.

The Bock's Best Series of Outstanding Piano Arrangements of Hymns and Gospel Songs by Fred Bock

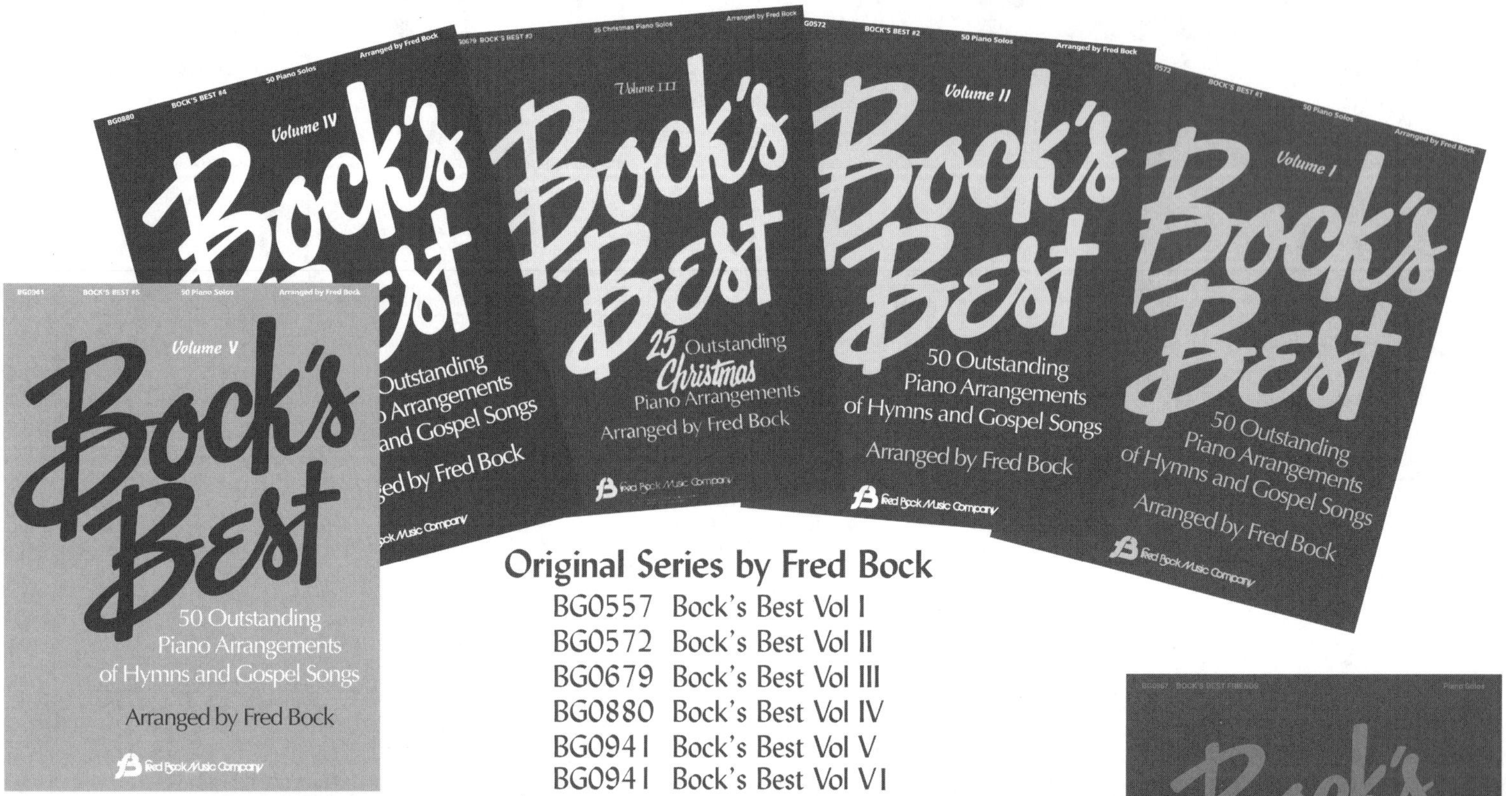

Original Series by Fred Bock

BG0557 Bock's Best Vol I
BG0572 Bock's Best Vol II
BG0679 Bock's Best Vol III
BG0880 Bock's Best Vol IV
BG0941 Bock's Best Vol V
BG0941 Bock's Best Vol VI

The E•Z Editions
adapted by Lloyd Larson

BG0991 E•Z Bock's Best Vol I
BGK1007 E•Z Bock's Best Vol II
BGK1012 E•Z Bock's Best Vol III
BGK1026 E•Z Bock's Best Vol IV

The Fred Bock Memorial Collection

Piano Solos in Celebration of the Life of Fred Bock Written by His Friends,
Stephen Nielson, Kurt Kaiser, Ken Medema, Bob Krogstad, Paul Johnson, Dwight Elrich, Jan Sanborn, Mark Hayes, William Phemister, Dick Bolks, Ted Cornell, Michele Murray, Ovid Young and Don Wyrtzen.

BG0967 Bock's Best Friends

Fred Bock Music Company

All are available at your favorite music store.